THE ANIMAL FILES
WE NEED
BUTTERFLIES

by Patricia Hutchison

FOCUS READERS

WWW.FOCUSREADERS.COM

Focus Readers is distributed by North Star Editions:
sales@northstareditions.com | 888-417-0195

Produced for Focus Readers by Red Line Editorial.

Content Consultant: David G. James, Associate Professor of Entomology, Washington State University

Photographs ©: Ogphoto/iStockphoto, cover, 1; Elenathewise/iStockphoto, 4–5; Gerald A. DeBoer/Shutterstock Images, 7; AM Padilla/Shutterstock Images, 9; Gerdzhikov/iStockphoto, 10–11; David Hosking/Science Source, 13; Seagull Photographic/Shutterstock Images, 15; Tom McHugh/Science Source, 16–17; MG photos/Shutterstock Images, 19; Red Line Editorial, 21, 29; JHVEPhoto/Shutterstock Images, 23; Ron Rowan Photography/Shutterstock Images, 24–25; Will & Deni McIntyre/Science Source, 27

Library of Congress Cataloging-in-Publication Data
Names: Hutchison, Patricia, author.
Title: We need butterflies / by Patricia Hutchison.
Description: Lake Elmo, MN : Focus Readers, [2019] | Series: The animal files
  | Audience: Grade 4 to 6. | Includes index.
Identifiers: LCCN 2018029250 (print) | LCCN 2018029507 (ebook) | ISBN
  9781641854856 (PDF) | ISBN 9781641854276 (ebook) | ISBN 9781641853118
  (hardcover : alk. paper) | ISBN 9781641853699 (paperback : alk. paper)
Subjects: LCSH: Butterflies--Ecology--Juvenile literature. |
  Butterflies--Conservation--Juvenile literature.
Classification: LCC QL544.2 (ebook) | LCC QL544.2 .H89 2019 (print) | DDC
  595.78/9--dc23
LC record available at https://lccn.loc.gov/2018029250

Printed in the United States of America
Mankato, MN
October, 2018

ABOUT THE AUTHOR

Patricia Hutchison is a former teacher. Since leaving the classroom, she enjoys writing books about science and social studies. She also loves traveling with her family, seeing new places, and studying nature.

TABLE OF CONTENTS

CHAPTER 1

COLORFUL HELPERS

A butterfly flutters in the wind. Its bright orange wings flash against the sky. The insect flies over a garden. Soon, it spots a daisy. The butterfly uses its legs to land softly on the petals. Then it straightens its coiled tongue. The tongue, called a proboscis, acts similar to a straw.

A monarch butterfly rests on a cluster of daisies.

The insect uses it to suck **nectar** from the flower. As the butterfly sips, **pollen** from the flower sticks to its legs. Then the butterfly moves to another flower. The pollen brushes off the butterfly's legs and falls onto the new flower. This process is called pollination. A pollinated flower makes seeds, which grow into new plants.

There are more than 17,000 species of butterflies in the world. They live on every continent except Antarctica. More than 75 percent of butterflies live in tropical regions. The world's butterflies come in many sizes and colors. Some butterflies' wingspans are less than 1 inch (2.5 cm). Others can grow to be

The western pygmy-blue is one of the smallest butterflies in the world.

almost 1 foot (0.3 m). Butterfly wings come in all colors of the rainbow.

Butterflies play a key role in nature. As they collect nectar, they pollinate flowers. Some butterflies fly over long distances.

They carry pollen to plants that are far apart. As a result, new plants grow in different places.

Butterflies have a major effect on Earth's food supply. The plants that butterflies pollinate provide food for many living things, including humans.

WARM WINGS

Butterflies are cold-blooded. Their body temperature changes with their surroundings. If they get too cold, they can't fly. This can become a problem when it is time to migrate. Thankfully, the sun helps. When the temperature drops, a butterfly lands on a sunny spot. Its wings soak up heat. The heat makes its way to the rest of the butterfly's body. Once the butterfly is warm, it takes off.

Cherry blossoms rely on animals such as butterflies and bees for pollination.

Farmers depend on pollinators to help their crops grow. Without pollinators, there would be no apples or chocolate. And many other foods could not grow.

CHAPTER 2

THE ROLES OF BUTTERFLIES

Butterflies do more than pollinate plants. They are also part of many food chains. A food chain shows the feeding relationships among animals. Birds, bats, lizards, and mice all eat butterflies. Butterflies make it easier for these animals to survive.

Many birds eat caterpillars and butterflies.

Butterflies also affect the growth of some bird populations. Butterflies begin life as caterpillars. Birds eat these caterpillars. Some birds only have babies when there are lots of caterpillars. That way, their chicks will have food to eat.

Butterflies help humans, too. For instance, they help scientists study **ecosystems**. Changes in an ecosystem affect butterflies quickly. By watching butterflies, scientists can figure out whether something is wrong in the ecosystem. Butterflies also have short lives. Many butterflies live less than two weeks. In this time, scientists can study a butterfly's full life span.

Scientists use nets to catch and study butterflies.

Butterflies also help scientists learn about other animals in the ecosystem. Butterflies are **invertebrates**. Roughly 97 percent of animal species on Earth are invertebrates. If butterflies are healthy, other invertebrates are likely to be healthy, too.

Butterflies can even warn scientists about **global warming**. As the planet gets warmer, some butterflies are moving to cooler areas. However, the planet may warm faster than butterflies can move.

ENERGY FROM THE SUN

Scientists used a microscope to study a swallowtail butterfly. The scales on the insect's wings were arranged like shingles on a roof. This pattern helps the butterfly take in heat from the sun. Scientists made a new **solar panel** based on the scales. They placed the panel's cells in a similar pattern. The new solar panel collects more energy from the sun than older panels. Solar energy creates less pollution than other energy sources. By polluting the planet less, humans can fight global warming.

Tiny scales make the swallowtail butterfly's wings colorful and strong.

If this happens, the butterflies could die.
Fewer butterflies leads to less pollination.
And less pollination leads to fewer plants.
If global warming worsens, its effects
could harm humans, too.

CHAPTER 3

A WORLD WITHOUT BUTTERFLIES

Threats to butterflies have grown in recent decades. Monarchs are especially in danger. There were nearly one billion fewer monarchs in 2015 than in 1990. **Habitat** loss is one of the main reasons for this disappearance. Builders often use chemicals to clear fields of plants. Then they build roads and houses.

The Xerces blue was one of the first American butterfly populations to die off from habitat loss.

Farmers also use chemicals to clear land. They destroy plants that butterflies need. For example, monarchs lay their eggs on milkweed plants. With fewer milkweed plants, monarchs lay fewer eggs. Over time, the monarch population falls.

Actions that help humans are not always good for butterflies. Putting out forest fires is one example. Forest fires can endanger people and homes. But fires also have benefits. They clear out old, diseased plants. Afterward, new plants, such as lupines, can grow. Karner blue butterflies need lupines to survive. They attach their eggs to the leaves. Later, the caterpillars eat the leaves. When humans

A Karner blue butterfly flies near a lupine plant.

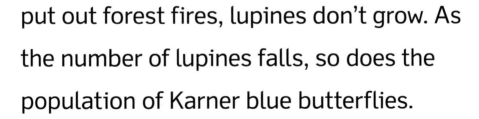

put out forest fires, lupines don't grow. As the number of lupines falls, so does the population of Karner blue butterflies.

Some butterfly species migrate north when the temperature becomes warmer.

But global warming may be affecting their migration. Global warming causes unusual shifts in temperature. Warm weather in late winter can cause an early migration. But if butterflies migrate too early, the weather might turn cold again. Many butterflies won't survive the cold weather. Global warming also causes droughts, or dry periods. Many plants die in droughts. As a result, butterflies have less food. This puts the butterflies at risk.

Declining butterfly populations can harm ecosystems. Many animals depend on butterflies for food. If butterfly populations fall, so will the number of birds, reptiles, and rodents. The air could also become more polluted. Plants take in carbon dioxide and give off oxygen. This process reduces air pollution. If pollinator populations decrease, there may be fewer plants to clean the air.

MONARCH MIGRATION ROUTES

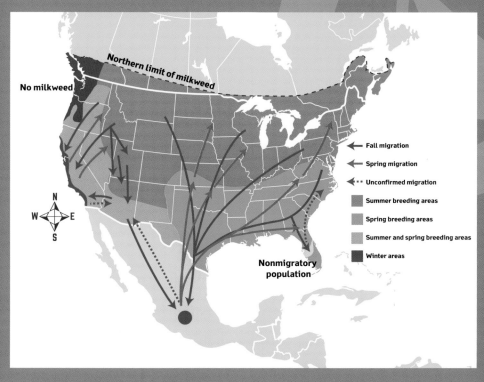

Northern limit of milkweed

No milkweed

→ Fall migration
→ Spring migration
⇠ Unconfirmed migration
Summer breeding areas
Spring breeding areas
Summer and spring breeding areas
Winter areas

Nonmigratory population

MONARCH MIGRATION

In the fall, days grow shorter and temperatures cool. These changes tell monarch butterflies that it's time to migrate. The monarchs fly south to find a warm place for winter. They fly up to 2,500 miles (4,020 km).

For most of the journey, the monarchs take many different paths. But in central Texas, they merge into a single flyway. After migrating for six to eight weeks, millions of monarchs arrive in central Mexico. They spend the winter resting in fir trees.

In the spring, the monarchs head back to Texas. They lay their eggs on milkweed plants. These eggs hatch into caterpillars. When the caterpillars become adult butterflies, they continue the journey north. After a few hundred

Migrating monarchs gather on a tree branch in Mexico.

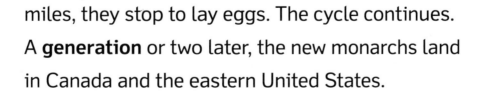

miles, they stop to lay eggs. The cycle continues.
A **generation** or two later, the new monarchs land
in Canada and the eastern United States.

CHAPTER 4

GIVING BACK TO BUTTERFLIES

The US Fish and Wildlife Service (FWS) wants to help monarch butterflies. This government organization teaches people about milkweed. The FWS gives out milkweed seeds for people to plant. That way, monarchs will have more places to lay eggs. People can plant the seeds in gardens, parks, or alongside roads.

A monarch caterpillar crawls across a milkweed plant.

There are many types of milkweed. Before planting, people should learn what kinds will grow in their area.

The Center for Biological Diversity thinks monarchs need better protection. This organization wants to add monarchs to the endangered species list. That way,

WORKING WITH ANIMALS

The US Fish and Wildlife Service works to protect animals and plants. Wildlife biologists work at the FWS. These workers study animals and their ecosystems. They also study humans' effects on wildlife. Wildlife biologists protect butterfly habitats. They teach people how to reduce the threats butterflies face.

Biologists put tags on butterflies so they can track and study them.

the species could get the protection it needs. In 2014, the organization sent a **petition** to the FWS. If the FWS approves the petition, monarchs would be listed as endangered. As of 2018, the FWS had not yet made a decision.

Anyone can help butterflies. To survive, butterflies need food and places to nest.

With that in mind, families can plant flowers to attract the insects. Butterflies will visit any garden, no matter how small. Even a plant on a windowsill can help.

People can learn about butterflies through butterfly **tourism**. Some towns have butterfly reserves. There, people can watch and study butterflies. In Mexico, there are several monarch reserves. On cold mornings, visitors watch the butterflies huddle in trees. Once the sun warms the insects, thousands take off. Tourists also learn about threats to monarchs.

Butterflies have existed for millions of years. Scientists think they survived the same extinction event that killed dinosaurs. Today, butterflies face a different challenge. Human activity is their greatest threat. Thankfully, helping butterflies is as easy as planting seeds.

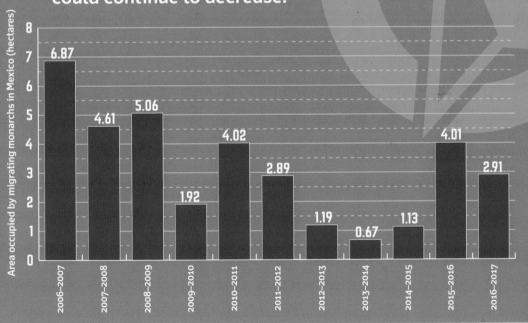

SAVING THE MONARCHS

If humans do not take action, monarch populations could continue to decrease.

Area occupied by migrating monarchs in Mexico (hectares)

Year	Value
2006–2007	6.87
2007–2008	4.61
2008–2009	5.06
2009–2010	1.92
2010–2011	4.02
2011–2012	2.89
2012–2013	1.19
2013–2014	0.67
2014–2015	1.13
2015–2016	4.01
2016–2017	2.91

FOCUS ON
BUTTERFLIES

Write your answers on a separate piece of paper.

1. Write a paragraph summarizing the main ideas of Chapter 2.

2. Do you think humans should put out forest fires? Why or why not?

3. Which butterflies need lupines to survive?

    A. monarchs
    B. swallowtails
    C. Karner blues

4. Which of the following human activities would be harmful to some monarch butterflies?

    A. planting milkweed
    B. cutting down forests
    C. using solar panels

Answer key on page 32.

GLOSSARY

ecosystems
The collections of living things in different natural areas.

generation
A group of people or animals born around the same time.

global warming
A long-term increase in the temperature of Earth's atmosphere caused by rising levels of pollution.

habitat
The type of place where plants or animals normally grow or live.

invertebrates
Animals that do not have backbones.

nectar
A sweet liquid released by plants.

petition
A formal request sent to an official person or group.

pollen
A fine powder produced by some plants.

solar panel
An object that converts the sun's energy into electricity.

tourism
When people visit an area for recreation.

TO LEARN MORE

BOOKS

Hirsch, Rebecca E. *The Monarchs Are Missing.* Minneapolis: Millbrook Press, 2018.

McCarthy, Cecilia Pinto. *Monarch Butterflies Matter.* Minneapolis: Abdo Publishing, 2016.

Sirota, Lyn. *Insects as Pollinators.* Vero Beach, FL: Rourke Educational Media, 2016.

NOTE TO EDUCATORS

Visit **www.focusreaders.com** to find lesson plans, activities, links, and other resources related to this title.

INDEX

Answer Key: 1. Answers will vary; **2.** Answers will vary; **3.** C; **4.** B